Caves of Chimera

AMERICAN AMARANTH

J. R. ORTIZ

ISBN: 0692880852

ISBN 13: 9780692880852

Library of Congress Control Number: 2017906309

AMERICAN AMARANTH LLC, Miami, FL

CAVES OF CHIMERA is a fictional play/narrative/novel/book of poetry.

Any resemblance of characters in the play/narrative/novel/book of poetry to real persons, living or dead, is purely coincidental and not intentional.

*THE SUN EXPLODED, EARTH ERUPTED,
AND ALL THINGS EVAPORATED IN A FLASH OF
BLINDING LIGHT*

Table of Contents

Prologue

S*apere aude*... The Latin phrase first used by Roman poet Horace in 20 BC - meaning 'Dare to know' - suggested the significant importance of wise persistence in human endeavor, and the need for strong and constant struggle in overcoming obstacles to attain virtuous goals. It was later used by the German philosopher Immanuel Kant in 1784 to describe the *Age of Enlightenment*, and the value of 'Reason' and intellectual liberty to solve the many complicated problems of humanity. *Sapere aude* urges us to think clearly, to discard the oppressive yoke of ignorance induced by oppressive society, and use our minds constructively with 'Uncommon Sense' to repair Man's common natures to be cruel and evil.

The Enlightenment dominated philosophical thought in 18th century Europe. Men like Voltaire, Rousseau, and Adam Smith proposed 'Reason' as the main source of authority; and advanced concepts like liberty, fraternity, scientific method, constitutional government, and religious tolerance. Americans - Benjamin Franklin, Thomas Jefferson, and James Madison – later incorporated many of the ideas into the *Declaration of Independence* and the *US Constitution*. The fields of science, law, sociology, and economics were greatly advanced during these years; and the thoughts of the Enlightenment were central to the American and French

revolutions. The doctrines and modern manufacturing pro-
cesses of the *Industrial Revolution* in the late 18th and early
19th centuries evolved directly from Enlightenment thinking.

The rise of modernity in the Western World led to the *Era
of Romanticism* (1800-1850) - an artistic, musical, and literary
movement emphasizing intense emotion, aesthetics, and
the glories of nature and the past. Romanticists believed art
and imagination raised the quality of human society. The
period was represented by many exceptional talents, includ-
ing: English poets – Wordsworth, Keats, Byron, and Shelley –
and painters Constable and Turner; French writers – Dumas
and Victor Hugo – and painter Delacroix; American novelists
- Edgar Allen Poe and Nathaniel Hawthorne – and painters
of the Hudson River School; Spanish painter Goya; German
music composers Beethoven, Schumann, and Wagner; and
Polish pianist Chopin.

Romantic thought also brought in an era of rising patri-
otic nationalism across Europe, which slowly evolved into
the horrors of the major world wars of the 20th century. From
Romanticism, the arts went initially into a *Period of Real-
ism* - where literature, painting, and sculpture depicted the
common realistic living conditions of Man; and then into a
progressive modern surreality and abstraction, essentially
nebulizing the real into whatever the viewer and reader
wished to see and feel. Fantasy and escape became the
central tenets of art.

The present modern world is a complicated one. There is
an unusual mixture of nationalism and global international-
ism across the planet. There is confusion in political thought,
journalism, science, economics, and the arts.

Today, there are also many countries armed and dan-
gerous. There are radical rebel terrorist groups too, openly

stating their international claims and belligerent ideologies. The Earth is a powder-keg of emotion and aggression.

Caves of Chimera, a long lyrical narrative poem, depicts a man and his family caught in an Armageddon Earth. A young father, Doctor Richard Planck – whose thinking mind is formed with philosophical elements of the Enlightenment, Romanticism, Realism, and modern Abstract Expressionism – returns to an idyllic mountain in northern Spain where he first learned love years before with a beautiful aspiring Spanish novelist. Through epic poetry, the reader learns of his emotions, experiences, and struggles in an absurd world.

Caves of Chimera

The deepest and darkest caverns in our lost minds…
No light, only sinister lurking forces and evil finds.
Creatures with sharp tooth and claw, black dragons,
capture and torture all benevolence – hitman assassins.

Crevices with death stench of dead and dying,
rotted corpses of last righteous warriors fighting.
Fire and dense arid smoke prevent easy breathing.
A floor of sharp steel spikes disallows free walking.

No leadership, no religion, no philosophy, no science, no art –
No chance to levitate inner spirits or energize sacred heart.
Massive cruel punishment in Satan pits of perdition underpart,
tied into a knot - vestige creative juice desires lost before
start.

World's only hope in clear thought armor of 'White Knight',
to light the flaming candles of *Veritas*, and bring truth to
darkness.
To sound music horn of the 'Good God', and paint color
foresight.
Recite healing poetry, and return sun and moon and stars
of kindness.

Reignite beauty of the *Caves of Chimera*, enlighten us from burden.
Show the way to new and sound prosperous horizon plateau station.
Locale of love and justice and reason – greed and cruelty unheard in.
Illuminate the dark corridors of Man's mind, liberate person and nation.

Illusion of Time

Time is only an illusion…
From *Big Bang* singularity
till *Big Rip* dissolution,
there is little inner clarity.

Universe measure of order to disorder,
progressive random entropy cosmic storm.
Explosive expansion to chaos limit border,
decline and loss of perfect physics form.

Ticking seconds in conscious mind -
Fast moves from present, to past and future.
Human time travel of neuronal kind -
Not knowing place in Space, never sure…

Origin light burst into infinite nothing -
Fertilized ovum zygote to multicellularity.
Giant mess unrest with nuclear aging -
Complications born from complexity.

Life systems, stellar and cellular -
Grow large, on to extreme peculiarity.
Withering clock delivers forms irregular -
A fading metamorphosis barbarity…

In our love – where does the chronometer stand?
Does it flow away, in a lost helpless way?
Or does it claim the great wished for land?
Oh my God! Oh my caring God! I say.

Allow me to seek soft notes of my senses,
the one peaceful kingdom of soul freedom,
kind tender beauty hum of cello finger stresses,
the color exposè of passion flower arboretum...

Alas... Throw away the illusion of Time curse!
I care not of my personal body extinction,
nor of the waves of dying matter of the universe,
nor of the dead stars' emission transmissions.

I only care for you and me, and everything we,
in this life, and any other we may ever see...
For you are everything in all of Time that be.
My only want is to be with thee, now and forever foresee...

Great Twisted Turning

Where does it come from, this angry homicidal evil stirring?
Repetitive fiery ambush along ascendance of Man Time -
Sinister vile black magic swirling, and unkind disturbing,
impeding good advancement of human social climb.

Sick foul-smelling excrement poisoning bestowed pure air,
over and over we see in our long and sad war history.
Exposing all wounding weakness into rabid cerebral despair,
altering divine workings of conferred sound mind chemistry.

How pathetically responsible we are, 'The Old and The Wise'…
Failing, hurting, and killing the beloved treasured young.
Forgetting their sacred spring flower rise, neglecting their cries,
damning and crushing their future dreams and hopes unsung.

Circular cycle eternal - in past with no merciful terminal end.
Today a final extinction threat, leaving the planet burning.
We must comprehend, and demand urgent a more conscious blend.
Make a strong unbending 'Last Stand' against the great twisted turning.

Black Hole

Vast legion armies of strong flesh and bone march into the black hole.
Tall boy combat zealots, soldier structure in fine color and plumed helmet.
Endless rows and columns robotic past flagpole, all under mind control.
Armed angry clenched teeth, steel glisten in air from infinite sharp bayonet.

War iron carriages with hot spewing muzzle roll into whirling spin drain.
Violent bellicose tank and rocket and cannon on fire, fall and disappear.
Tools of slut inhumane council brain, pulled down into Lucifer's domain.
No bringer of glory dawn or morning star, only dark hatred and sick fear.

Women and children refugee stare alone into field of intense time gravity.
No lucid light; only gloom, grim doom, and shadow; no safe easy escape.
They too stumble wounded into bloody death pit, a chaos vortex insanity.
Genocide of scarred innocent masses, no pure survivors of Earth's devil rape.

Churn turns of Man history, awful futile repetitions and depraved retakes.

Lack of sufficient vision virtue, or kind chance to console hurting soul.

Endless outbreak and quakes, too many costly mindless mistakes.

Suck and sink of God's holy humanity into the profane wretched black hole.

Ashes of Aphrodite

Born of spirit castration, queen goddess of love and beauty.
Supreme sensuous pleasure nude, arising from green sea foam.
Nubile and fertile, grand rivalry for favors in lands of king realty.
Arriving at shore, shiny virgin pearl on upturned scallop shell dome.

Not a rose or dove or swan of peace, but a desirable red apple.
Men of high power fight to the death for unique and sultry gifts.
Gambling fate and destiny to the wind, risking throne and castle.
Willing to collapse State, and set their unknowing people adrifts.

Long tug-of-war and conflict, using weapons of all mass destruction.
Piling dead bodies and cursing souls, in complete disregard of humanity.
Civil abduction and truth obstruction, and even genocide instruction -
An utter shame of conduction, in disgraceful and scandalous infamy.

For ultimate senseless treasure riches, a race of criminal desperadoes.

Blind and deaf to acts of tolerance and sympathy, hateful of God Almighty.

Oblivious to throes and lamentations, and holy echoes of wise old heroes.

We the abandoned, on our long road of sorrows - in the ashes of Aphrodite.

Effusions in Conscious Mind

With sparks from strikes of flint on pyrite,
bright tinder fire births light from stone.
No slow mind appetite, only strong catabolite -
We all wish to express, define, and atone.

Struggle to show humane from inhumane -
Specks of truth in seas void of eternal verity.
From a demented world domain in total disdain -
In all rarity, genuine traces of clarity and charity.

To remain real in the morass of insignificance,
to create and beautify from glory mankind.
In labored dissonance of Sisyphus – diligence.
Streams of good calm effusions in conscious mind.

Take Me There

Take me there…
To that special singular exhilarating place.
That high luscious plateau, only you and I know.
Where I alone hear your voice, and see your face.
A far away love paradise, only you and I can go.

Into the other world of seldom seen long lost horizon.
Infinitely lithe private line in the mind, all royal blue.
Where conjoined free spirit and soul forever rise in -
A heaven divine rendezvous, our own Xanadu…

Bodies pressed melt close, strong beat - heart to heart.
Lips in heat locked entwine, your warm breath in mine.
State of fever euphoria, a red performance art apart.
Gazing stars hush content, in grand blush combine.

Bounty glory light, all radiant white.
Red magenta fires in distant glow.
The blind Earth, closed eyesight.
Peace angels chanting, wish it so.

Into 'Essence Time Almighty',
into high exquisite thin air fair,
onto realm of true and worthy Aphrodite -
Take me there…

Reflections of You

I sense you deep, in all I realize...
In distant untouchable sky, melt into land -
Blue and green mixing peace, as in your eyes...
On lonely tranquil beaches, in every grain of sand.

In steps on colored stone, crossing mountain brook;
and cool fresh water past my fingers atop the Earth.
In every word of every love poem in our favorite book.
In night to dawn, and the sun's calm early birth.

In sound of wind, restless through arms and legs of trees;
and princess dance of tall green grasses in same sweet
blow.
In the soft gentle touch of my face by a warm ocean breeze,
and quiet radiant beauty of long silent full moon's glow.

In yellow and lavender color splashes of hillside lilies,
and exotic display of giant orchids and tiny primrose.
In butterflies and bumblebees, and all birds, eye sees.
Alluring notes of romantic ballad we can compose.

In scent of baby flower, springing onto the world;
and visible drops of morning dew in all fields of view.
Whirled into magical dream, a content life unfurled.
In all I see and ever saw, I only sense reflections of you...

ACT I

— ⊶⊷ —

Inspiration

I t was a shadowy and threatening wind. A 'Black Death' shroud enveloped me in a twirling tornado of sharp knives and steel spikes, pinning me motionless against cold ancient limestone of my beloved medieval church at the base of *Monte Chimera*. Hopeless and lifeless, the airs of screaming ghosts and infernal ghouls were drawn from the deepest bowels of the earth…

I rested against the basilica, covered in soot and ash. I was short of breath with fever and productive cough; my lungs and insides were dying rapidly. I could feel my cells mutating, and not regenerating normally to heal damages done two weeks earlier.

I bent over in pain and vomited the few salty crackers I had eaten an hour ago. Mixed in was a glob of bright red bloody tissue.

I struggled into the church and sat to rest. Lit clear by a thousand burning candles, a large crucifix rose from the ground in front of me. It held a wooden body of Jesus, from floor to ceiling. I prayed...

An old priest in black cassock came to me. His clerical cloth was tattered and beaten by the angry elements. His white hair and beard were dirty, and his face was dusted with grime.

"*¿De donde eres, hijo mio?*" He muttered in tired Spanish voice.

"I am sorry, Father... I speak a poor *Castellano*," I said.

"Where are you from, my son?" asked the priest in clear English.

"Nowhere, and everywhere..." I answered slowly.

I stared up at the stained glass windows. The flashing light show in the sky outside created an artful strobe depiction of the story. They were scenes of Man's 'Fall from Grace'. People's faces expressed horror and terror. Their tossed bodies seemed to writhe in agony. The bright and beautiful colors of the glass did not soften the tale told.

"The alienation of Man from God," the priest said softly... "His damnation."

"How prophetic..." I whispered.

"We could see it coming even a millennium ago," sighed the old priest.

I lowered my head in grief. Composing myself, I said gently, "I was married in this church, Father, twenty years ago. It is kind to see that it still stands."

"It will never fall, my son... It will be here for you always."

"Thank you, Father," I cried...

The priest moved away silently, leaving me alone in thought. He seemed to disappear into nothing, as all our lives had done.

I returned to the wicked outdoors. I swigged water from my last bottle and stared up at the Cantabrian peak. The rock appeared solid against the swirling grey and black clouds full of white lightning. Streaks of red crimson and bold cobalt blue light shot through the devil skyscape in short bursts like machine gun fire. Bullets of fluorescent green tracers sparked in angry nature's crazy wild background. I was here to rise into that Luciferian nightmare. My Valhalla sat near the top of *Chimera.*

My arms and legs were covered with blotchy purple purpura, skin signs of low platelets from a sick bone marrow. A large non-healing wound in my forearm exuded greenish yellow pus, indicating white blood cells were succumbing to vengeful bacteria attempting to take over on this new Earth. I had studied medicine and practiced pediatric surgery. I had seen these signs before in my leukemia patients.

I closed my eyes and took a deep breath, aching from every rib. I wondered what had happened to my once beautiful dreamy 'Green Spain'. I remembered the emerald valleys and rich woodlands from visits in the past. I had treasured the turquoise sea and ever-changing panoramic sky, the green hillsides and colorful flower fields. Hikes into the mountains of *Chimera* had been treks into heaven.

I called out for my son, above the stony outcropping. I needed his hand. My legs were weak and trembling. Anemic muscle tissues were oxygen starved...

"Grab tight, Father!" He shouted, above the roar of rushing air around us. He pulled me up into a small dug-out of rock at the base of *Monte Chimera*, a large monolith rising in a chain of mountains in northern Spain, a few miles from the Bay of Biscay.

"It's so damned cold!" I said loud and clear into my son Joseph's ear, before clearing away from the wind.

"It's late August, Father... The coldest August in thousands of years, I'm sure."

"Stay covered up, Joey... Give a blanket to Leslie. She looks as cold as I am."

Leslie was Joseph's girlfriend from school back home in England. They were both seventeen and strong, and still bright eyed and handsome kids. Joey had grown to a big man, with dark hair and light eyes. He had chiseled features like his gorgeous mother. Leslie was blonde and beautiful. Both had been fine athletes.

We all huddled into the small stony hole and built a small fire with deadwood from the nearby forest. We passed around a large box of raisins, and shared crackers and cheese given to us by a gracious old woman villager in the town of *Chimera* earlier in the day. We covered ourselves in blankets.

"What time is it?" I asked Joey.

"Four in the afternoon, Father. But it's already night with the sun blocked out by the ash clouds."

"The wind is shifting to the west. Hopefully, by morning we'll see some light," I said.

"Is that ash from England, Doctor Planck?" Asked the scared and quiet Leslie.

"I don't know, girl... perhaps... It could be coming from Paris, or further east in Germany... Impossible to know for sure..."

"How do you feel, Father? Do you think you'll be able to make it up another thousand feet? It's very steep..."

"I believe so, Son. I've been up this trail many times. I'll make it up this time too."

Joseph looked at me with deep sad eyes. He knew this time was different. My illness was clear to him. He understood the situation.

"I'll make sure you make it up, Dad…"

I could sense in him a determination to help me. If he had to, he'd carry me up all the way, dead or alive.

"I can count on you, Joey," I smiled.

"Why was that old lady staying in *Chimera*, and not moving south like everyone else?" Asked Leslie. "She seemed at peace, staying in her tiny house alone, not having anyone to defend her."

"People in these mountains have lived in their villages all their lives," I stated. "Usually for generations, families have enjoyed a serene quiet country life, free of any hardships or dangers. At her age, she's not afraid to die in the only home she's known.

"Besides, how could she possibly figure out the craziness of this world and know where it could be safer?"

"Is there any place safe, Dad?"

I looked at Joey hard. "Maybe to the south," I said, "near the Mediterranean Spanish coast, or across to North Africa."

"North Africa?" Asked an incredulous Joseph with a gasp.

"If it's safer, go there," I stared.

"And America, Father?"

"I don't believe you should consider a near-future in America, Joey… Can't be certain, with communications as they are, but I suspect it's hellacious there right now. It'd be safer in the southern extremes of Europe. Last we heard, before leaving southern England, the U.S. was devastated.

"If you can make it to New Zealand somehow, I'd go. But it's far, and there won't be any regular forms of travel to get there.

"Stay on the southern coast of Spain until things improve, Joey... Promise me, Son..."

"I will, Father."

"And take good care of this girl," I smiled at Leslie. "She's too pretty to leave alone at the party."

The teen-agers held hands and embraced. I held them both in my arms.

"Now let's get some sleep before morning," I suggested...

The children rested into unconsciousness, and I watched. The soft low light of our lantern shadowed their quiet bodies against the rock of our dugout. Occasionally, one would flinch in a nightmare scare; but they rested more than me. My painful insides kept me awake.

I searched through my backpack for a painkiller. On our way south to the coast of England, I'd been able to secure some antibiotics, analgesics, anti-emetics and anti-diarrheal medications, and iodine tablets and vitamins for the kids from a ransacked small town pharmacy. We'd also taken some canned food and bottled water.

In the bag too was my pistol and a small box of ammunition, which I had remembered to take from my car before abandoning it. I quietly placed the gun into my son's backpack.

Surrounded by torrid hellish winds outside, I turned off the lantern. After a while, the pain lessened and I was also able to sleep into my nightmares...

We awakened early, in the dim light of our new world, and began our ascent of *Monte Chimera*. We rose above a ridge line and onto a still green hillside. The narrow valley was framed by steep massive white cliffs. A rushing river ran through the middle of it. North, we could see a dull livid pastel blue-grey sky and Cantabrian sea mix with each other without clear border. A pale sun in the east appeared as a faded light bulb in dense haze.

A dark fog blurred the forest rising before us, allowing only a glimpse of the upper reaches of denuded trees. The mist emanated from the woodlands and engulfed us in an eerie white, grey, and black silence.

Joseph, in the lead, stopped and pointed. Streaming past us in opposite direction was a column of people in different states of physical decay. Men and women of all ages, and children also, stumbled out of the mysterious forest like torpid stiffs. None spoke, and they all had bewildered looks with empty faces and sunken eyes. We observed them as they passed, one by one; afraid to ask from where they had come, or to where they were going.

In the thick blinding mist, one of the cadaver men wore a 'Med School' t-shirt. He was young, but appeared unhealthier than the rest.

"Are you American?" I shouted out.

"Yes..." He mumbled.

"Are you a doctor?"

"Yes," he said, before falling to the ground.

My son and I helped him to sit.

"Where are you coming from?" I asked, holding his back.

"France... We've been walking for ten days. The mountain crossing of the Pyrenees was brutal. We lost many on the trek to bandits and the elements."

"What's the state of government in France?" I enquired.

"There is none... There is no longer an official France... After the bombing of Paris, martial order was declared. But it was unsustainable. The army disbanded. Hordes of raving mad men roam the streets of cities and towns, raping and pillaging. There have been many atrocities. Millions have died."

"And the hospitals?" I asked, giving him a sip of water.

"None are operational, without electricity and with few doctors and nurses."

"Have you heard of America?" I asked in fear.

"In Paris, we heard of many strikes on population centers in the United States. All major cities were wiped from the map," he stated with jumbled words, catching his breath.

I glared at my son and Leslie. We had heard similar news in England.

"Where does your group intend to go?" Blurted Joseph.

"Southern Spain... The still intact Spanish government has fought an African uprising there, and established a safe zone with lodging and medicines. It's our only hope!" Screamed the man, before collapsing.

Two male streamers grabbed at my backpack. Joseph pulled the pistol and drove them away, still in silence.

We left the dead American on the ground and continued our hike into the hidden forest...

Quiet and blanketed in a grey cloud, the land was petrified. All green color had disappeared, leaving only black tree trunks and brittle leafless broken branches poking into the air. There was no sound of life, without even the hoot of an owl or rustle of a ground squirrel. Old 'Green Spain' had been poisoned.

We continued our climb along a footpath, stopping to rest on a rocky ledge overlooking the sea. I had been here before.

With great fatigue, I took several deep breaths. I knew it would only be a short distance to our destination. I was almost there.

Leslie helped remove my rucksack, before settling down. The air was clearer, and we could see the expanse of ocean to the north. A dense smog obscured the valley below us.

"Are you alright, Doctor Planck?" Asked Leslie.

"I'll be fine," I said.

Leslie and Joseph sat holding hands, looking concerned for me.

"We're close... Just a little bit more," I assured.

"You certainly know your way, Father."

"I've been here many times, Joseph; as you have been. It's been a long while, but you don't ever forget," I softly voiced.

I had come to this flat rock outlook over the sea many times with Elizabeth. We had first kissed here, and made love. She had read me gentle poetry in this special place, viewing the blue blue sea and green green hillsides. In memory, the flat rock was a most sacred site, full of life and love...

I thought back many years, and a smile came to my face. Though in great pain, my soul felt enriched and complete...

"Do you hold any hope, Father?"

"I do for you and Leslie. Simply follow my advice and move south. I suspect the Spanish officials there will maintain some order."

My son nodded his head. "No Father, I mean for you?"

"No, Joseph... I'm done... The damages are irreversible..."

"It's a good thing, you and Leslie were in the school basement at the time of the blast. You were just far enough also, to prevent acute radiation effects. The iodine pills will help reduce the risk of thyroid mutations and neoplasia."

My son embraced me.

"I love you, Father..."

"I love you both," I said.

"What occurred?" Questioned Joseph, bewildered by the chaotic circumstances. "How could all this happen?"

"We'll never know," I answered slowly. "We'll never know who shot first or last, or why... Man became careless and overconfident. Responsible nations became irresponsible. Bad leadership enveloped the absurd world. Terrorist organizations acquired nuclear weapons. There were too many bad actors to keep track of the insane geopolitics and social dynamics. In retrospect, it was practically unavoidable.

"Noble America became corrupt... The workings of government, financial institutions, big industry, the corporations, the decrepit health care system... The process failed the American people. We lost our righteous humility, sane virtuous judgement, and just behavior... How could we police the world when we couldn't police even ourselves?

"The whys aren't important any longer... It's too late for that... Human survival in a primitive landscape will be the challenge from now on... You must live through this, Joey, without losing spirit and the creative self," I pressed, looking into his eyes with all the energy I had remaining.

"Do you think we'll make it, Doctor Planck?" Asked a nervous Leslie.

"You both are young, strong, and in love... That's all you need," I promised.

"And Mother and John?" Asked a sad Joseph. "What were your last words, Father?"

John was my other cherished son, twin brother of Joseph. He had been kept from school for several days because of a nagging respiratory infection. His mother was caring for him at our home in central London.

Joseph had just started his senior year at a boarding school, an hour's drive from the city. At the time of the detonation, I was on my way to visit him.

Crazy Man had forsaken my beloved family and had abandoned the world. In all his hubris, he had forgotten the delicate balance of human nature and peace on the planet. The 'savage' mind had taken over reason and sound management. The order of the day became total destruction and a suicidal sense of right and wrong.

"My dear, dear John," I muttered to myself. "I miss you so…"

"Lay back, Doctor Planck," pleaded Leslie, placing her jacket behind my head against the hard stone.

My son came and sat next to me. He held my hand firmly.

"Your mother and I had decided to leave London, with all the recent domestic unrest and rioting. International relations had worsened to the point of pending calamity. We sensed it coming. All countries had lost their heads. Military escalation everywhere had made conflict inevitable.

"I was on my way to pick you up…

"We were all to leave south the next day, to our friend's coastal airfield. We planned to fly to Cantabria and lodge up for a while until the situation had cleared, one way or the other.

"My friend got us here eventually, on his old turboprop… But without your mother and John," I grieved…

"I was miles from London on the highway, speaking to Mother on the phone. She was packing and making final arrangements for departure in the morning.

"Then we heard the attack sirens. The same ones that had been tested all week, directing us to the tube tunnels.

"After a short silence on the phone, your mother said, 'Oh God, I think this time's for real... I love you, Richard,' she whispered tenderly with her sweet voice.

"There was a sharp loud shrill before the phone ceased. The car stalled...

"Then, like the sun exploding, an extraordinary fearsome bright light blanched white everything around me. It was followed immediately by a thunderous roar of the earth splitting in half. A great wind came, pushing cars off the road and into each other. My auto was thrown into a ditch against a trailer truck. Through my shattered windshield, I could see people flying in the air past me. At a distance, a giant black mushroom cloud rose above the city.

"The raging winds subsided. I exited the car and attempted to help the torn and suffering. Many people had died in the smashups. A heavy black ash rain covered the highway, making breathing almost impossible. There weren't many survivors. After a short time, it was evident London had been pulverized and millions had died. The few of us still standing, like zombies in stricken horror, continued moving south away from the city.

"By the next morning, I had walked all the way to your school. I was happy to see you both safe in the basement lower level. The headmaster was quick in his decisions. He followed the instructions perfectly. He saved many lives."

"You too, Father... I heard stories in the medical field station you organized... You cared for hundreds of survivors. Most of them lived."

"The volunteers made the difference," I said. "Although the thermal burn cases from the outskirts of London will die shortly, I believe.

"I did all I could, Joseph; but then, I also became ill…"

"I know, Father… Now rest… Please rest…"

"She said she loved me, but I had no time to say anything… No time to comfort her," I mumbled, before going into a deep sleep…

I Saw You, and I Knew

At old outdoor café, under a lemon-yellow umbrella,
on a warm breezy summer morning with bluest open sky,
surrounded by vibrant purple and red and pink *buganvilla*,
and tall spires of sierra, like stone church towers mighty high.

Smell of espresso coffee and breakfast in fresh air,
sounds of Spanish guitar romance strings and songs.
Heart music, and aromas for the senses everywhere.
A place in town square, whither joy spirit belongs.

At table nearby, with white vintage sun hat and rose plume.
Red ruby full lips, ravishing glamour face and soulful eyes.
Long bare legs, and body swoon of sensuous goddess in
bloom.
Beauty ideal to tempt and hypnotize - all desires arise.

In wonder glare, I sat aroused by magnificent splendor of
thee.
A high grace luminosity in hand movements and serene
pose.
And more... A radiant glow rarity of fine simple soul sincerity.
Embedded force presence, to where great love flows and
grows.

I stepped to your side like star-struck boy, and asked a favor. To share a bite and chilled wine, and share pleasant stories too.

Without waiver, you accepted; each to the other becoming savior.

I gazed deep into true Spanish eyes... I saw you, and I knew...

On Green Hillside

We walked close - hand in hand – on green hillside,
by deep broad-leaved forest in white gorge limestone,
along flower filled meadow and wide turquoise seaside,
near singing skylark, sparrow and swallow in woodland own.

With fields of violet trumpet gentian, bluebell, and purple thistle,
yellow dandelion and daisy in rich emerald river valley gleam.
Mountain pond reflecting azure sky, with warm wind flow ripple,
alpine butterfly and Iberian lizard sunbathing by twisted stream.

To lay and rest below steep massive massif, thousand feet high,
amongst hidden Cantabrian bear and wolf animal lust energy,
sharing swirl of great wine in glass, nature beauty nearby.
All in all, great fancy in mind and body, thick stimulant synergy.

On green hillside, sight of fine fair lady stripped naked skin white.
Hot-blood thoroughbred broodmare, with thick black hair in a tail.
Virgin body oiled in nature, tanning strong in mid-day solar power light.
Senses surround, bathed in fantastic pheromone wash of phenom female.

Tantalize, sparkle and shine – never fade ever presence of your eyes divine.

Roman goddess nose and cream pink lips, enveloping rapture tongue of Venus.

My vision crystalline on breast mounds and backside, down *linea alba* supine.

Waistline hips, erotic vigor of fleshy loin, sensuous legs and feet between us.

Under majesty of romantic *Monte Chimera*, in wild robust affair sierra.

Where sun and moon never set, and stars of Zeus in heavens collide.

Bodies entwine, motion and grind, sweat off our backs on *firma tierra*.

Love in the Spanish afternoon, in soft short grass, on green hillside…

Eyes That See

I awaken on cool green grass of spring to summer.
Nature's early light falls warm on breast and brow.
Wonder of color, sky and flower, now so recover.
Blue above, and aside – rose and daffodil yellow row.

Body stripped bare, only skin and hair, all too fair.
Mind vast and open to wishful hope and dream.
In fresh thin air with Cupid's care, profound affair.
Gentle love wind blow by stony mountain stream.

I hold your hand, and lay my sight in marvel feast.
Restless thoughts of carnal beauty pass through me.
Wrapped by life splendor, evoked by lust of beast,
I fall in blessed trance – beholden to my eyes that see…

Unspoken Word

In the fine piercing glint of your eye,
and color flash of the look and lash,
shy sweet solemn sighs under blue sky.
Galloping hearts in dash whiplash...

In your tender smile power sovereign,
and lush lips of dripping silk and honey,
torrid flows of feeling so uncommon,
a mystic ride in other-worldly journey...

In your blessed touch of shock electric,
and luminous heights of devoted spirit soar,
towards tower of majestic poet centric,
adore and adore to almighty sacred core...

In slow forever tick-tock of holy Time sublime,
in unheard surreal, with margins blurred,
in supreme ideal passion marrow prime,
with love on the tongue in unspoken word...

Always in Your Kiss

It was always in your kiss...
That secret explosion of song and light,
enchanted sweet hiss of amorous bliss,
roaring height of bright star rocket flight.

Pounding power of dual heartbeat,
and throb of my member extreme.
Penetrant unison of our red carnal heat.
Wet stream flow and tribal scream.

Afterglow of tender love possession,
and soft breath blow on warm lips.
Deep impression of euphoric expression,
and calm soothing touch of your fingertips.

Wrap of your arms around my chest,
your pulsing hips in still rhythmic kinesis.
Tightly pressed flesh dance, breast to breast.
Yet, the secret was always in your kiss...

A Persistence of You and I

In all times past, and in times present,
there is a fine persistence of you and I.
Together we, in grand ascent and descent,
always there, as moons and stars pass by...

Traces of us in all lucid memory see,
in great songs and dance and poetry.
In blue seas, and green hills, in all that be.
Our close and placid spirit form, alive and free.

A wondrous spell bound force of nature say.
Power of magic love intense fervent.
Totality imbued in passion potion spray.
Each to the other, inspired romance servant.

Hope and pray for golden fortune destiny.
Your hand in mine, in sky without cry.
To have and to hold, to cherish so preciously,
and forever fly - a persistence of you and I...

Visage

In the *visage* of your face - I see,
eyes soulful and penetrant into me.
Mind and grace of a *bel esprit*,
devotion and love of ultimate degree...

From your beloved look - I hear,
rings of countless church bells,
words of romance – poetic Shakespeare,
songs of passion desire – no parallels...

With the turn of your head - I feel,
charm enchanter golden arrow of *Erato*,
warm ideal of soul companion real.
I forever, your hardwood timber inamorato...

In your wondrous one-and-only smile - I live,
timeless, with no end to our starry cosmos.
With heart felt wishes of only my love to give,
in my remembrance, *visage* of you was most...

In a World Insincere, There is You

In lieu of unhinged aberrant social dystonia, there is you.
There is ballet where there was demented spastic contraction.
Rather hatred and abuse, there is true love and joy breakthrough.
Sweet gentle violins in place of ugly banging drum subtraction.

In you, I view my devoted holy spirit world apart -
engulfed by light, pink passion flower and song.
Captured in warm ring of fire – sacred heart.
I breathe free and easy, alive in vigor, I so belong.

In you, winters are not cold and summers hot.
The days are not long and hard, but too fast.
Our red strings of fate tied tight in love knot.
Dreams last, old past expectations surpassed.

In you, night sky and sea are more blue, and stars bright.
Day sun shines stronger without burn, a mellow yellow.
The moonglow stills the dark, in sight of angel white.
No loud noise bellow, only strings of soft tender cello.

In you, mortal pulse quickens into galloping horse.
There is lively strength of amorous muscle flesh.
My source spring fountain of never-ending carnal force.
A sensory invigoration of the earth in me, all things afresh.

In you, there is no falling Time, no fret of distress hourglass.
Caught in forever frame without name, eternal spirit flame.
Power singularity - a universe center of mass without trespass,
where cherubs joy exclaim, and vile forces of treachery
tame.

In you, I am blind and deaf and dumb to upturned silly
sphere.
Worry and trouble fade invisible, personal complication too.
There is elation, triumph, and rejoice even in last sorrow tear.
With great fear and confusion in a world insincere – there is
you...

ACT II

---⊶⊷---

Hold of Breath

had come to the north coast of Spain for the first time. Just finished with medical school, I had a few weeks to relax before beginning my residency training. I expected seven long and grueling years to become a pediatric surgeon.

My concept of relaxation was different from most people. I was in Cantabria to cliff dive *El Coronel* into the Bay of Biscay, and to hike the rugged seaside mountains. Always an adventurer, I'd been all over the world in search of physical challenges.

A friend in college had once spoken of the dangerous white rocky platform, where Nationalist troops had thrown a Republican colonel into the ocean to his death during the Spanish Civil War. Few persons had attempted the dive as an exercise, although the rock had seen many suicides. I wanted to feel the thrill of flying fists first from 125 feet into the cool waters of the Cantabrian Sea.

After walking the long wide pale sand beach and climbing the steep side of the mountain, I arrived atop the flat stone before noon and the high sun. The rough coastline was desolate of people. I was alone.

Stripped bare, I stood near the edge and looked out over the blue bay waters. Strong frothy white waves crashed the shore to the sides of *El Coronel*. The vertical dive would be into a relatively still pool, protected from the sea by thick perimeter rocks. I'd enter twenty foot depths at more than fifty-five miles per hour.

All my life, friends had considered me strange for liking such desperate things. I'd usually explain away the dare-devil behavior with morbid jokes and funny comments. But in truth, I knew better. I understood my interests were dangerous.

In the end, I'd always think, what did it matter? I had grown up against all odds, from nothing; and at final tally, we all went to nothing anyway. I had no family, and I changed girlfriends like underwear. No one was dependent on me yet. I enjoyed the excitement of not knowing the outcome. It was all about the thrill.

I had learned well my college physics. Life and knowledge had hardened me more than most of my colleagues. It seemed the more I knew, the more reckless I became.

From an infinitely small single cosmic quantum 'Origin Point', matter made from nothing had crashed with anti-matter and produced an explosive expansion of a universe. All things were born of the clash, and spread across an imponderable and immeasurable vastness of never-ending borderless 'Space'. All flowed and disappeared into the blackness. Ever accelerating outward, eventually all objects would lose view of each other.

I wanted my heartbeat fast in this 'Great Unknown'. I wished to live and experience everything with energy before the void...

I stretched out and limbered my body. My muscles were sore from the day before. I had made several practice dives off a smaller cliff nearby.

I looked up at the sun. Through the cool wind, the powerful radiant shine felt good on my naked body. I stepped to the precipice and gazed out, not down. The turquoise sea was a beautiful sight, with its whitecaps and distant sailing ships. I took a deep breath and plunged...

The next morning, I set out on mountain bike from my rented small stone house on a green hill by the Bay of Biscay. On country road, I imbibed the stunning scenery of deep green valleys filled with fields of colorful flowers and quaint red-roofed farm villages. The majestic tall white limestone peaks nearly touched the bluest sky I'd ever seen. Beside me flowed a rushing river to the sea.

I stopped for breakfast in *Chimera*, attracted by its old church and plaza. Centuries old, the town had a special look and feel. Its central square was full of potted flowers, and surrounding terraces were draped in red and purple *buganvilla*.

I sat at an unshaded table of the outdoor café by an old used book store, where I had purchased *Le Mythe de Sisyphe* by the French philosopher Albert Camus. In scent of strong coffee and food, I began to turn pages.

While reading, I was distracted by the fresh gardenia fragrance of a lady's perfume. Looking up, I caught a first glimpse of her.

Nearby under a bright yellow umbrella, wearing a white sun hat with rose plume, sat the most marvelous woman of creation. As she spoke with her server, chatting away with a giant smile, I could only stare.

Her heaven face could stop the Earth's rotation, with red ruby lips and soulful sapphire eyes graced by a hint of mint. Her long sensuous bare arms and legs, and elegant hands and sandaled feet, mesmerized me as they danced in speech. She was a bolero ballet in motion, a Spanish goddess.

The beauty saw me gazing. She turned away and smiled in irresistible blush, just before an opportune gust of wind set her hat in flight.

Retrieving my great fortune, I came to her...

"*Buen dia, jovencita,*" I said in newly learned Spanish, delicately returning her hat.

"Thank you," she responded in British English with a Venetian smile.

"You are English?" I asked politely.

"Only half... My father is Spanish."

"And you? Are you American?" She enquired, putting her hat to the side and leaving me to mentally wander through her gorgeous long wind-swept black hair.

"Yes," I fumbled, trying to concentrate; but falling again as she crossed her legs to the other side and exposed muscular thigh.

"Would you like to share a bite and a glass of chilled wine?" I asked slowly.

"Certainly," she agreed as I sat beside her.

"You are into Camus and the absurd world," she pointed with her fine nose... "There is no absurd struggle in Green Spain," the goddess laughed; "only beauty and music and love..."

A man in the small plaza began playing a romantic ballad on guitar.

"There is struggle in everything, and all things may have an absurd side," I stated, slightly embarrassed and placing the book in my backpack.

"That may be true, but I choose to look at things in a different way," she said softly...

"What do you do?" asked the Madonna.

"I studied medicine in America and graduated only a few weeks ago. I plan to be a pediatric surgeon."

"I hope you won't find absurdity in that," she laughed.

"I will relish in the struggle," I responded.

"So it's the struggle that allows you to deal with the absurdity of existence," she retorted.

"Perhaps, and a few other things," I smiled...

"What is your name, Girl?"

"Elizabeth Carreno... And you, *Muchacho*?"

"Richard... Richard Planck..."

Coming closer to her, without allowing my heartbeat to be heard, "What are you doing in this small village?"

"I write novels about young people in love... I've come here to research my next story. I live nearby in Bilbao."

"Love stories... Is there ever absurdity in that?" I asked.

"I don't believe so... Not in true love," she batted her eyes...

We ordered wine and early lunch. While we waited, we spoke of Cantabria and Spain. She told me of her years at Cambridge studying literature and English romantic poetry.

Two young girls approached our table and asked Elizabeth to sign their book. The thick novel was titled, *Heartwind*. The girls expressed their great admiration and devotion to her unique writing style.

"It seems popular," I said.

"It won some awards, and British television is creating a miniseries," Elizabeth hushed. "But I don't like thinking too much of my successes."

"So there is a little of Camus in you too," I jokingly stressed... "What is the story of *Heartwind*?"

"It is difficult for me to explain my novels... Read it when you return to America."

I peered into her deep eyes and said tenderly, "I will..."

I got a room at the small hotel in the square, unwilling to leave *Chimera* and the wonderful Elizabeth. She was near at a rented apartment. We both could hear the guitar from the plaza with our windows open.

After a few days of eating breakfast, lunch and dinner together, and briskly walking the town and countryside, we spent the evenings and mornings making love. We would discuss philosophy and poetry and the making of the world. Only rarely would we speak of science and medicine and the rigors of academia. Pleasure, in all its forms, seemed always on our tongues and in our spirits. We became enveloped in a cocoon of kind sensuality with fierce physical love-making. In the warm days, our sexual sweat would soak the bed; and in the late nights with guitar in our ears, our breasts and brows would be cooled from their fever.

"Why did you come to Cantabria?" Asked Elizabeth, as I lay beside her naked body on a crisp morning.

I didn't answer at first, pressing my hands on her flesh. I passed my fingers between her thighs and felt her gush. I tasted her breasts and loved her more...

"*El Coronel*," I murmured.

"The deadly cliff on the coast?"

"Yes, the killer dive… I dove from the top the second day after arriving…"

"You mean a fresh medical graduate with a bright future healing sick children, full of love and passion, traveled thousands of miles to jump off a steep mountain into a turbulent sea?"

"I didn't jump… I dove headfirst," I expressed emphatically.

"Why would anyone want to do that? Risk life in a physical struggle? Why a suicidal death wish in a person with so much to live for?"

"It's my make-up, Elizabeth… I can't give you a logical reason for always wanting a struggle. My mind and body are always in a fight with something. At times, I can't find an enemy; and I'll create one for purpose of the struggle. I live in combat; without it, I am dead."

"Oh… You are so different from me, Richard… You don't know how to relish the peace and serenity of being alive in this wonderful world. I see beauty and calm in all. Songs, stories, visual art – They are all reflections of the 'Good Soul'. Why search for violence and physical calamity, when surrounded by such grace and natural wonder… I don't believe in tempting the devil…"

"You don't understand, Elizabeth."

"Yes, I do… Testosterone can poison the minds of some men, and can lead to unwise and dangerous actions and events. Certain women can fall also.

"You must come from nothing," she said.

I drew back from her. She had touched a raw nerve…

"I lost my parents as a child… I grew up in foster homes with rough friends. But I worked and studied hard. I was given a chance with academic scholarships, and I made it. I survived…

"I'd prefer to speak no more of this."

"There will be no struggle with me, Richard."

I gazed into her eyes with the passion of a lone tiger in the woods searching for a mate. I pushed my thumb past her ruby lips against her warm tongue, and then kissed her strongly. I firmed my member into her even more strongly.

"The only struggle with you for me will be the inability to suppress my desires and instincts to always be in you... To love you with my body and mind equally... To keep from suffocating you with my love..." I said softly...

That afternoon we rode bikes back to my stone seaside cottage on a green hill overlooking the Bay of Biscay. It was isolated alone on the hill, without neighbors. Made of pale limestone, the small house had a fireplace and large windows facing north to the sea.

In the evening, with a warm fire blazing, we sat naked for dinner. We drank our red wine as we ate, always gazing into each other with love and lust. Our shadows were cast on stone beside us, like flickering ghost spirits.

"Are you going to tell me of *Heartwind*?" I asked gently.

"No," said Elizabeth, clinking my glass...

"Why not?"

"Writers can't speak of love in their stories, Richard... It's too sacred for them. I wish the reader their own interpretation. I write what I see in my mind and feel. It's too hard to explain past thoughts and emotions. If I tried to explain, the same feelings I sensed when writing could not be expressed. It is better to keep quiet and allow the story to speak for itself."

"Why do you write about love?" I asked.

"Why did you study medicine? And now wish to piece together broken children, Richard? Isn't everything all about love?

"In order to get the marrow of life, you must reach the soul... And the way to the soul is through love..."

"But do you bare your own soul in the writing?" I enquired.

"Do you not bare your own soul, Richard, in the saving of the sick and dying?

"In all worthy endeavor, in all things of true value for humanity, the doer must open the deepest and most sacred spaces of their being. We are resurrected every time we do so...

"So yes, Richard... I bare myself... I open my heart and soul, the totality of my existence, in every word of every line of every story I write... I must get the reader to see things clearly, and learn to seize opportunity when love knocks at their door."

"So the author keeps no secrets?" I asked.

"The secrets are in the thoughts, Richard, of the writer and reader; they are not in the words written..."

Early the next day, Elizabeth and I walked the long pale beach below the hill. It was a windy and cloudy cool morning. The seabirds seemed to stand still as they flew. The long green grasses on sand dunes danced in the flowing air.

The sun was hazy in the grey sky, like a distant light in a fog. Wearing thick sweaters, we walked warm in each other's arms.

"Have you ever loved, Richard?"

"Not until now," I confirmed... "And you?"

"I have loved only in my dreams," she whispered into my ear, her words muffled by rough air and the cries of seagulls.

A rush and spray of seawater suddenly shot into the sky over us, drenching me. Elizabeth had escaped the cold bath by racing up onto a sand dune.

"Are you cold, Richard?" She laughed loudly.

"Freezing!" I shouted...

"Now look at me!" She ordered in command.

"Stop and stare at me with your life, Richard!

"Feel the wind on your back? Is it cold?"

"I'm frozen solid!" I screamed.

"Keep looking at me... Do you love me?" She asked.

Stopped in my tracks on the cool sand, with a cold rushing tide around me, and the freezing wind at my back; I stared in loving wonder of the girl I adored.

"Are you still cold?" She asked gently.

"No!" I shouted... "The sight of you warms me, Elizabeth... The sea wind no longer feels cold."

She smiled at me from the dune, with a power unspoken in word. Her golden heart and light had warmed the wind around me, enveloping me in her love.

"Now you know, Richard, the power of *Heartwind*; It is here for us..."

We returned to the town of *Chimera* in the afternoon, and stopped to eat at an old village inn at the bottom of *El Monte*. A middle aged woman served us beer and a delicious meal of veal and lobster.

"I see you are equipped for a long hike into the Spanish hills," she smiled... "You are lovers... No?"

Elizabeth and I smiled back.

"Yes... We are lovers," affirmed Elizabeth.

"Then you both must eat a hearty meal to give great energy, to prepare for love making. You will enjoy the thick green grass carpets of our hillsides. The ground is soft and accommodating," she laughed, pouring us more beer.

"Yes! You must eat and drink and be merry!" She shouted, waving at her young son to play guitar.

"Have you been to *Monte Chimera* before?" Asked the woman.

"I have," answered Elizabeth.

"With this bull?" pointed the woman at me with pursed lips.

"Alone," laughed Elizabeth, hugging me.

"Alone in *Chimera*? I cannot believe that! You cannot make love to yourself, Girl!" Shouted our server, bringing us more bread.

"My sons have impregnated many women in these hills. These mountains are for robust people to explore and discover. This is a rugged land for rugged love and soft poetry, for song and dance, for full relish of life.

"And also, of course, you must make love in our secret caves, surrounded by the ancient glories of *Chimera*," advised the woman.

"What caves of glories?" Inquired Elizabeth.

"Oh! I must not tell," said the woman... "Those are secrets you must find on your own, if God so wishes."

"We have three days to experience the monte," I said.

"You only need a minute to find the glories I speak of, if it is so intended... If you do, I assure you will return many times. The power is too great to forget. Once seen, the walls of the caves call you back. You will make many babies here," grinned the server, singing her way to the kitchen...

After a full night's rest, we began our hike into the hills. Elizabeth had told me of the beauties of lush valleys and mountain streams. The large fields of colorful flowers and farm pastures seemed to never end. The forests were rich and deep, with tall trees full of leaves.

The day's sun was interrupted for minutes with a cool rain drizzle, misting our faces with sweet freshness. A rainbow arched over a river valley, directing us to our next green hillside; where we lunched good food and drank good wine, before stripping bare and making love to exhaustion in bright daylight.

In our evenings under the stars, we'd recite poetry to each other and sing old Spanish folk songs taught to me by Elizabeth. We slept little and loved much.

On our last morning, on a verdant idyllic hillside, with direct views to the blue sea and *El Coronel*, with the white-caps of distant waves fading into a lost horizon, Elizabeth held my hand.

"Do you have family, Richard?"

"I'm not even sure of my last name, Elizabeth... As I understand, my father was an adventurer who worked for the US government overseas. He'd come around our home once in a while to visit with my mother and me. I don't really remember him. One day, he just disappeared forever. Soon after, my mother committed suicide. I was young, and don't recollect any details. I entered the foster home system until I was old enough to strike out on my own. And here I am, Doctor Richard Planck..."

Elizabeth broke out crying. I held her in my arms until she stopped.

In the late afternoon, we began our descent along a narrow ridgeline of *Monte Chimera*. Below us, like an Impressionist canvas of pastel yellows and pinks and reds, with green pastures across a wonder landscape from Heaven, the beauty of the world shouted out in joy. We stopped on our path many times to breathe in the glory airs of Cantabria.

Then, like the luring song of a fair vestal virgin guarding the sacred fires of virtue, we heard the wind. A secret sonorous air flowed from between rocks on the ground to our ears, stopping us in mid-stride...

From Earth to Heaven

On rising verdant valley, climbing stone spire -
a walk with you in sacred solitary rapture.
Remote fierce tigers in land inspiration fire -
free souls gripped tight, spirit force capture.

Travel high, my woman and I, to white rock sky chapels -
on bountiful fertile pasture, all filled with glories of God.
In land of wisdom tree, knowledge, and forbidden apples -
from my naked rib, love grows against serpent flawed.

Mind journey procession – treacherous and dark - unkind;
perhaps better noted as voyage of fine obsession expression,
long grand tour subconscious creation of unconfined
mankind.
One world to next, towards Elysium - from Earth to Heaven…

Fall from Grace

In tall fall from sacred grace,
from hallowed eminent domain –
to cold empty solitary place,
where no careful minds sustain...

From high pillared regal forum,
to pitted battleground scarred,
with loss of human decorum,
no spirit guard – all surface marred...

Insane greed and envy too great,
need for unrivaled power scorned.
No directed conscience - - too late - -
Now forewarned extinction mourned...

Why slip from fruitful color Eden?
Wicked collapse, no thoughtful reason,
mighty implosion from serene peace start,
crumble crash meltdown - neglect of art...

For cause and effect – 'Black Hand' search ends.
Wide turn to pseudo-human machination,
a drama of robotic lifeless animation extends - -
Cessation of good passion soul creation...

Thus, the prodigal Homo Sapiens downfall...
From gates of Heaven Hall, to beyond infernal wall,
down to dirty earthy soil and hungry insect crawl,
beneath old green and sun - way down dead below all...

Man of Holy Trinity, founder of own ugly demise -
lost in solo cyanotic Space of no good comfort advice,
with no soft sea breezes or clear light for tired eyes,
with no white full moon, and no more breathless sunrise...

Firestorm

Why?
From where does this devastation derive?
Where is humanity cry, as we sit and die?
What happened to our strive and thrive?

Good science and medicine for every citizen,
brainpower empathy for humble civility,
world search for rare righteous discipline,
growth of sensible moral elasticity...

In vast universe, in all eternal parallel universes -
amongst sacred billions of billions of hot suns,
through countless infinite planetary intersperses,
in forever numbers of unimaginable life runs...

This Earth, this singular unique fantastic Earth - -
Born of natural explosive collision gravity pull,
rotating on delicate axis in God's grand scheme worth,
orbiting power star along heavenly path full...

Living gardens, breathing plants and animals galore.
Air and water synchronicity in Time and Space.
Life special central core, tho in constant Darwinian war.
Everywhere – danger interface in touch with human race...

Oh Man! Oh, little Man!
From where are we born?
From Garden of Eden ban?
Or from monkey and tree limb torn?

We must consider more, and love more.
We must look profound within ourselves.
Find and open lost total freedom door.
Reach high for wisdom bookshelves...

Into nobility and gentility, no crazy futility.
No mad mind and matter to final degree.
The sane cannot allow such insensibility.
Stand and fight, don't flee from 'Flame Tree'...

Rise! Awaken deepest spirits! Open souls!
Bold in action, sharpen fast creative form.
Sight fine virtue, lofty peace goals.
Cast away hate and greed - avoid wicked firestorm...

Sad Eyes

If your eyes were a canvas – I'd paint a picture...
Indigo sea, and tiny boats near shore with bold colored sails.
White sand beach, and awe mountain backdrop special mixture.
Bright golden sun beaming on foggy hidden trails...

Steep green valley with rapid river to blue sweep.
Flower fields in every color to match a rainbow in the sky.
Grand beauty in all direction, dreamscape memory keep.
Tranquil peace, inspire and beating heart glorify...

I'd drop you from 'angel yard', onto our secret paradise,
under shade of tree by aqua creek on rolling hillside.
Your beloved image surreal, with margins imprecise.
Your love waiting for me, arms and heart open wide...

All I can do to enrich our life, persist to see your kind smile.
To make permanent bond eternal -- avoid goodbyes.
Hold your hand forever, in our deserved spirit exile.
Kiss you soft and long, and return our joy into sad eyes...

Heartwind

Climbing to mountaintop, your heartwind at my back -
with internal solace and hopeful sense of reuniting.
Remembrance past, of flower lilac and star tender zodiac.
Existence in haze - no forward end or before beginning.

Every labored step I take, you are gentle within me.
Every hazard turn and stumble make, every breath.
In every last wild orchid and solid oak tree I see.
Oh! My dear dear darling, my sweet sweet Elizabeth.

Unjust it all is, in deep darkness and grey of day.
Mornings of falling ash, no rich green grass wet with dew.
A confused and crazy world took you and our son away,
and sent atomic wind to weaken - but fill too, my sails to
you.

Afternoons without warm shine and ray of crisp sun.
Evening stars blotted black across now nowhere sky.
Sorrow and anger disbelief, hate for what was done.
To see all ever beauty wither, all lovely life die.

Torment frigid harsh airs blow, sad tears flow.
An agony steady and fierce, all respite rescind.
Image glow of you and me, and family - wished so.
And compassionate love caress of your heartwind...

Tabernacles of Faith

High above the range, above green hills into foggy cloud,
first and last white rock chapels of hope and faith – exhibitions to Man.
Unknown creative labyrinths, hidden millennia in darkness shroud,
where humankind passed sincerest thought through epoch span.

Long parade of pigment banners on stone, collecting over years;
grand museum of abstract form -- circles, triangles, and squares.
Holy show of animal and plant, of river and sky, wishes and fears;
the gentle people -- their hearts and hands, and inner cares.

Depictions of beings caught in trial and tribulation – tests of fortitude.
Waves of unforgiving climate danger, famine, epidemic, and tribal war.
But also, temples of rich love to show art in adoration and gratitude -
where soul mankind was born and reborn, with sacred spirit outpour.

'Saga' history unfolds, with many more returns to holy *Chimera*;

to further story told - to etch and sculpt, and paint truth emotion force;

to collect great mental works of art, in every angel and devil era.

Tabernacles of faith – our first and last depository of mindful resource.

On This White Soft Stone, I Leave

On this white soft stone, I leave -
traces of gelid ages past and gone,
of great color gardens of Adam and Eve,
and astral pink and blue topaz dawn.

Of long walks through deep forest green,
and savage crossings of cold rivers swift;
of stunning treks traverse serene ravine,
under warm foggy summer rain mist gift.

Of land with sunflowers rising to the sky,
with fields of fruit and grain - and beasts of pride;
of ocean shore bounty aplenty to satisfy,
a life ideal by majestic mountain seaside.

To show and share with you and ours,
fantastic tales of epic Man we weave;
of creative hours and visual powers,
on this white soft stone, I leave...

Tremble Song

I trembled at the gentle sound of your voice.
Heard a symphony of a thousand strings.
Violins sang sweet love song of rejoice.
Melody heart and soul sprang wings...

Chorus tender brought joy and ecstasy.
Ring and chime of bells swooned bliss.
Notes danced to my ear in rhapsody.
Word music composed into a deep kiss.

Away! Away with regret, worry, and doubt!
You gave me felicity, a warm paradise glory.
Splendor nirvana! Even sound asleep, I'd shout.
Halcyon days, immersed in profound love story.

Alas! Life changed... That was then, now is now.
I long in sorrow weep for my kind dream choice.
Cannot live without – in endless seek somehow.
I sadly miss the soft tremble song of your voice.

ACT III

―――∞∞∞―――

Expiration

fell against the stones, injuring my side. It did not matter anymore - another wound, one more sore, one more pain. I had finally arrived at my last place, my destination of permanency.

"Father... Are you alright?" Asked a concerned Joseph, helping me from the ground.

"Doctor Planck!" Distressed Leslie, watching but unable to move.

I sat on a small boulder, and rested my head back. Though the sun was rising, it was dull and cold. It was certain to be another windy and dark day in 'Green Spain'.

Joseph gave me water and chocolate for energy. The 'old woman' in *Chimera*, the same who had served Elizabeth and me at the village inn years ago - before our first ascent of *El Monte*, had supplied us with bites to eat.

Leslie passed a wet cloth across my forehead and around my eyes. She pressed it against my side to staunch bleeding.

"There's blood coming from everywhere," she cried.

Joseph wrapped a bandage around me, padding wounds with gauze.

"It's okay," I said... "Push the rocks, Joseph! Open the cave!"

I helped my son with my feet, pushing as hard as I could. Leslie also assisted with all her strength.

Twelve large stones were moved out of the way, revealing a man-sized black hole entrance into the summit of *Monte Chimera*. The cave opening was even darker than our surroundings.

Joseph shined his flashlight on a footpath he and his brother had traversed several times as young children. It had been more than ten years since his last visit.

"Do you remember the way, Joey?" I asked...

He looked into the cavern with big eyes. "Yes, Father... I remember... I remember every last step."

"Give the light to Leslie, and help me up. I need to get to the end. It's a long walk, at least a thousand feet," I said in exhausted voice.

"We both can help," stated the girl, getting under my right arm.

We stepped slowly into the cave together. Joseph pulled a lantern from my rucksack and raised it into the still air. We could sense the expanse of the high stone ceiling above us.

"It's big!" Declared an awed Leslie, pointing her light to the top.

"It's more than big!" Echoed Joseph.

"Keep walking, Kids," I implored.

The *Caves of Chimera* were an interconnected maze of stony corridors and large vestibule antechambers leading into even larger spaces. A cool stream of crystal water ran through most of the system, opening into small ponds filled with blind fish. The air was much warmer than the outer environment, and there were no noxious fumes.

I was able to walk on my own, and directed the children further into the vault. We passed through three separate halls, finally arriving into the first major inner chamber. I stopped to rest by a water basin.

"Look at those fish!" Shouted Leslie… "They are white like snow, and have no eyes!"

"They don't need eyes in the dark!" Laughed Joseph.

I dipped my cupped hands into the water and drank. It felt cool and fresh as it had in the past.

"Fill the bottles, Joey… You'll need them for the trip south… It's safe to drink," I guaranteed.

"Can we bathe in it?" He asked.

"Yeah! But after you fill the bottles, and take some fish for breakfast!" I snapped jokingly.

Joey pulled deadwood from his pack and started a small fire. Leslie netted several fish. I filleted them clean, looking away as the young people jumped naked into the water. I had done the same many times here. It was their turn now…

It felt comfortable and safe inside the caves. There was no violent wind or thunder, or scary skylights. There was no ash rain or ugly smells in the air. You could almost forget all the hell we'd been through.

We sat down to eat, although I had no appetite. The sound of running water next to me was calming.

"I never gave these critters to you and your brother to eat... Did I?"

"I don't remember, Father... It was a long time ago... But they sure taste good," grinned Joseph.

"Anything fresh and not in a wrapper tastes fine," said the girl.

"Make certain you take some south. It'll be okay to ingest for a couple of days. Save the packaged food for later," I stressed.

"What is it about these caves that drew you back so many times, Doctor Planck?" Asked a curious Leslie.

"Joseph hasn't told you?" I enquired.

"No... He hasn't shared a word," she said, peering over at my son.

Joey turned the light to the low ceiling right above Leslie's head. She gazed up.

"Oh my God," spoke Leslie...

She slowly rose to her feet and passed her fingers across the stone, touching the deep purple color of an ancient cave painting. The depicted bison with horns spread across the ceiling for nearly ten feet. Made of earth pigments, the clay ochre, charcoal, and ground calcite had been mixed with cave water and animal blood and fat. Sensitive and thoughtful paleolithic fingers had then pressed and smeared the pigments onto the limestone wall of the *Caves of Chimera*.

"This is amazing," quietly sighed Leslie, entranced by the beauty above her.

Joseph passed the light further across, showing his girl a long procession of varied animals. Cave bears and wild cats, hyenas, deer, and horses paraded in long murals on walls and ceiling, deep into the inner walkways of the cave. Mainly in red and black, and using the contours of the rock surface, the three-dimensional figures of all sizes were clear and detailed. Eyes and ears, teeth, horns, and tails were well defined. They seemed painted yesterday.

"They are tens of thousands of years old, Leslie..." I said. "You are looking at the dawn of art, the oldest paintings in the world - an ancient art museum of Stone Age Man.

"Elizabeth and I called this chamber, 'The Gallery of Animals'. Primitive artists spent days working on these masterpieces. They are the first signs of creative human intelligence. They poured their spirits into the images. These were the creatures that provided nourishment, and some also represented predatory dangers. Their lives were entwined with these beasts.

"Look over there, Leslie, in the rocky alcove by the second pool. Get close to the painting.

"You're viewing, most likely, the first dramatic representation in the history of visual art.

"It shows a forest scene, where a woman has been eviscerated by a lion. Her lifeless body is surrounded by little animals of the woods, observing as spectators of nature. The woman's intestines are growing out from her into the living environment, like roots of young growing trees and blossoming spring flowers. Above the remains is her ghost in pink and peach color, embraced by her lonely sad male lover in blue. The pictorial represents the struggles of Man and Mother Nature, and the eternal cycle of life and death on Earth...

"When first seeing that masterpiece, Elizabeth and I were moved to tears. We could not believe ancient Man could have such dramatic emotion. I suspect it may be the greatest work of art on Earth...

"My wife and I thought the images in the caves had been painted in series, over many different epochs. There may perhaps be ten to fifteen thousand years of work here. Many tribes of peoples, each passing their time before going away, placed their fingers on these soft limestone walls. Famines, climate disasters, epidemics, and wars would take their tolls on the tribes and the creations of the caves. These works are a pictorial essay on the evolution of civilization.

"Elizabeth and I discovered this wonder by pure accident. We came back many times over the years, never revealing its location to anyone. We were selfish, realizing public revelation would eventually lead to its closing – just like all the other ancient cave galleries of Europe. We didn't want to relinquish our access. It was too special for us.

"Joseph and his brother were brought several times in their early lives... They enjoyed swimming in the pools..."

"Why haven't you returned in the past ten years, Doctor Planck?" Innocently asked Leslie, looking over at Joseph.

My son grasped his girl's hand.

"Beatriz," he said softly... "My older sister, Beatriz... After she died, we never came back."

"You've never spoken of her to me," regretted the girl.

"No... No, I haven't," answered my son in subdued undertone...

Joseph led Leslie along the walls of the chamber, explaining every detail like his mother and I had explained to him as a child. The girl's eyes were curious and excited. She asked many questions as her mind raced through all the spectacular renderings of ancient life in northern Spain.

I silently followed the young people, allowing them to bond together in delight as I had with Elizabeth. The beauty of the art was really expressed through the communal emotion of sharing with someone you loved. Regardless of the awful calamitous conditions outside the caves, the incredible power of sensitive and creative thoughtfulness inside the caves produced an overwhelming euphoria. The elation of the beauty overtook your senses in an avalanche of kind introspection. You felt protected by the art...

We walked into another chamber. "The Gallery of Land Forms," I said...

The immense heights of the walls were filled with images of glaciers, mountains and valleys, rivers, and stands of tall tree forests. Fields of wildflowers in different shades of yellow and red covered a narrow hall into the next chamber. The ceiling exhibited white star constellations and the different phases of the moon.

"The Gallery of Geometric Shapes!" Exclaimed Joseph... "Every abstract form is shown in this section of the caves. Squares, rectangles, triangles, circles, and dots of varying sizes are mixed into different sketches of early geometry. Parallel and perpendicular lines form images similar to those you'd find on architectural plans. These were the thoughts of budding builders."

I struggled. Thoughts of Beatriz filled my mind. Our lovely and wonderful daughter had died at age ten. Elizabeth and I, and my sons, never recovered from the painful loss. She had been the light of our eyes.

Great dizziness and fatigue overwhelmed my body. I could barely take a breath. Radiation poisoning had taken out my ability to produce blood cells. A dead bone marrow, and failing brain and cardiorespiratory systems had caught up with me. I needed to arrive soon at the final gallery.

I slipped and fell again to the ground, entering the next big space. Joseph helped me sit opposite a giant mural. The wall in front was fifty feet across, and rose at least two dozen more. The lower half of the painting was charcoal black, the upper a bright sulfuric yellow. In the center of the painting, a large impressive red outline of a primitive human figure stood with hands raised in offering.

"The Hall of Truth," I hushed into my son's ear. "From darkness, into light," I said in a weak voice.

"Yes, Father... The 'Truth'... Always fight for the 'Truth'... Don't worry any longer... I will remember..."

"Man falls so easily into deceit and greed," I declared. "We are failed beings... We forget the honor of being alive. We lose ourselves in the chase of false hopes and dreams. The struggle must be just and good. Love of all life, respect for all life, devotion to the glory of life must be at the heart core of the journey. Our steps on the sacred path must be measured in goodness. Fight for this 'Truth' to your last breath. Grow strong and courageous in the endeavor, Joseph. Don't be like most... Live with a bold sense of enlightened romantic realism. Use progressive abstract thought, out of the box, to rebuild a more sensible position for Man on Earth.

"Many years ago, I dove off the top of *El Coronel*. Standing firm on the platform, looking down on the wind tossed sea and white crashes of waves against rocks, I wondered if I'd live another minute. I wrestled with death in my mind, as a gladiator prepares to meet an angry and hungry lion. I promised myself, if I'd live, I would strive even harder in life and vanquish every obstacle. But more importantly, I told myself that tomorrow would be a kind day, and every day thereafter would be finer… The next morning, I met your mother…

"Always rise to the 'Truth'… From shadow, to the sun," I encouraged.

Leslie began to weep. In the low light of the lantern, I could still see her tears flow and lips tremble.

"No distress, Child… Empower yourself in the *Caves of Chimera*. Here lies the very essence of Man. Take it into your soul. Use its energy to survive and rise again. Fear not…

"Now, help me into the 'Hall of Hands', Joseph," I demanded.

My strong son carried me to the end of the last chamber. We were surrounded by hundreds of painted hand images. Some were solid imprints, others were outlines created with blow pipes made from hollow animal bone tubes. The hands of men, women, and children, in all colors, filled the stone room.

"Light the candle from my backpack," I gently ordered, as I lay on the hard floor. I softly touched a set of handprints, isolated from the rest.

"Here, Father…"

Joseph placed the candle between me and the images. A flickering low white glow allowed my fingers to trace the outlines of the hands. I lovingly touched every digit of each hand…

"These are ours, Joseph… Your mother and I… Beatriz, you and John… From many years ago…

"I have loved you all, with all…

"Your mother saved me, you know… At the beginning, and many times more… She changed my life… I adored her…

"This is what I have left… A set of five handprints, on a limestone wall in a cave of northern 'Green Spain', created in very happy times, long ago…"

I looked into my son's eyes. I could sense his mourning for me.

"I am sorry, Joseph, for losing Beatriz…

"It was a simple appendix, like the countless others I had performed. Her life seemed to slip away from me. I fought so hard to bring her back… So very hard," I repeated…

I stared again at the stone wall. Next to the hands of my beloved family, aside the precious handprints of my darling Beatriz, was a small ancient painting. Most likely drawn by a juvenile, it had always been Elizabeth's favorite. The simple head and body figures of several young children - in bright and colorful purple, orange, pink, and blue – were bathed in the radiant yellow luminance of the sun. Beatriz had named the masterpiece, *Children of the Stars*…

"The *Caves of Chimera*," I said in a loving voice… "It is here where I wish my bones to be for eternity…"

Doctor Richard Planck pulled his son close, and whispered into his ear. He then took a final breath, before settling beside the glories of *Chimera*.

Joseph cradled his father, softly kissing his face. Leslie stood behind, bowing her head. The hours passed…

The young adults made their way out of the caves. Another dull and dark morning was breaking. The hazy rising sun was topped by a sky of ominous flashing greens, and reds, and lavender pinks. In a patch of clear, a bright round light with a fiery tail flew through the airs.

Joseph pointed high with his finger.

"A sailing comet... *Un aviso del cielo*, like the Spanish say – a sign from Heaven!" He shouted.

Embracing her boy, Leslie delicately asked, "What did your father whisper at the end?"

A brave and bold Joseph peered into the foggy and dark valley below. He then stared up into the atomic aurora, before slowly turning his gaze to the streaking comet in the small stretch of clear sky...

The composed boy kissed his girl on the lips, passing his gentle fingers through her hair, and said in a very tender and profound way - "Start over..."

Epilogue

Atomic Aurora

Slow energy flows of red crimson and gold.
In swirl wash of smoke, dark grey and black.
Hot streaks, bright green and blue bold.
White flashes, nuclear light tracks in attack.

Sky alive with orange fire ember.
Flying twinkle sparks in waves of ash.
All dead matter, life forms forever never.
Organic tissues burn, incinerator mash.

Roar of whirling wind, sound of fury.
Resonance through town and country.
Noise of power crash upon valley.
Counter fond nature's jury and story.

Strong electric ozone smell of oxide fill,
and grill scent of living carbon combust.
No fragrance from rose or Spanish daffodil.
No aromas of briny sea or woodland forest.

Even in the dastardly, in human tragedy insane.
In horror actions, Man evil doings gone profane.

Ugly brain's bane, and awful pain of millions slain.
I have visions of beauty too, of love persist, of you...

In chilly airy winds, frightful shooting color lights.
Smoke and grey of day, hazy hopeless starless nights.
Fear of deadly nuclear lightning strikes, demonic sights.
I see mind images of restful peace, of serene calm, of you...

In abhorrent sounds of coming death, freedom loss obscene.
End of life shrill, terrible terror, human rights demean.
Man gone filthy mad, immoral revolt, music killing machine.
I still hear the *amor* song, a soft gentle melody, of you...

In fetid perish malodor, putrid fatal tomb fume stink.
Loss of fragrant splendor flower fields – all yellow, red, and pink.
Disappearance of things kind glory scent, all beauty link.
I still sense the love bouquet, elegant bloom perfume, of you...

In shocking display of total human destruction - atomic aurora.
In loss of all first and last light, all joy glow of universal life aura.
Extinction of God's creation fauna and flora – evils of box Pandora.
I still see and feel you in all, inherit you into soul emotion from all -
And love you forevermore...

Acknowledgements

IN THE FINE WORLD, I SEE
WHERE ALL KIND BEAUTY BE
ATOP ALL BLUE IS ONLY YOU
AND MY SINCEREST LOVE TOO

www.ingramcontent.com/pod-product-compliance
Lightning Source LLC
Chambersburg PA
CBHW031524040426
42445CB00009B/383